Living THE Days OF Lent 2011

Anita M. Constance, SC

Paulist Press
New York / Mahwah, NJ

ISBN 978-0-8091-4658-1

Published by Paulist Press
997 Macarthur Boulevard
Mahwah, New Jersey 07430

www.paulistpress.com

Printed and bound in the
United States of America

Introduction

During Lent, the church invites us to make the journey inward. Our destination is God. Our path is transformation. Conversion depends upon our commitment and God's grace. Yet, it is the grace of God that keeps us in the direction of our desire and goal. We are drawn toward the Light, toward Jesus, aware of our shadow but never overcome by its darkness. Sin is not so much a turning away from the light as it is a refusal to advance. But necessity pushes us where virtue has not yet led.

God is always aware of us, always aware of what is still unhealed. In Jesus Christ, God embraces our human limitations. Through him, God untiringly reaches out, and so we turn with confidence knowing God has already turned to us. This is a journey we will make again and again. We were not born in pieces, but it takes a lifetime to discover our wholeness—the fullness of God's original intention. Let us continue the journey...once again.

—Anita M. Constance, SC

Hastening Holiness

"Beware of practicing your piety before others in order to be seen by them;...when you give alms, do not let your left hand know what your right hand is doing....Whenever you pray, go into your room and shut the door and pray to your Father...when you fast...[groom your hair] and wash your face...."
—Matthew 6:1–6, 16–17

We turn round, O God, and round and round each year, each day in search of our home which is you. You are a gracious host, patient with our wanderings, steadfast with blessings at an open door.

Cast compassion before us as crumbs, that we might find our way to you. Wash away the guilt that burdens us with fear and faltering steps. Turn our eyes toward you; grant us a depth of vision that sees into your heart and celebrates the sleight of hand. May our prayers abandon city streets for the quiet corners of truth, and there may we be held fast by Jesus whose embrace graced the cross and hastened holiness home. Amen.

What is lost to my eyes is found in God's vision.

Readings: Joel 2:12–18; Psalm 51; 2 Corinthians 5:20—6:2; Matthew 6:1–6, 16–18

Freedom to Follow

"If any want to become my followers, let them deny themselves and take up their cross daily and follow me. For those who want to save their life will lose it, and those who lose their life for my sake will save it."
—Luke 9:23–24

God of fullness, you blessed our lives with choices and opportunities. How gracious your gift of freedom—birthed in our beginnings, fleshed-out on the path between life and death.

Your call to life is held in delicate balance on the beams of a cross. Your gift of hope rests in the roots of that tree where we ponder the wisdom of lost and found. Followers of a crucified Christ, we are tempted to drag our feet. Suffering and rejection are bitter pills from the physician of new life.

God of our longing, free us from ourselves. May your invitation to mystery encourage the risk-taking. Remind us that to follow is child-meekness; to lose, the threshold of finding; and to die, the dawn of eternal life. Amen.

Commitment does not come easily. "Yes" is never spoken without struggle.

Readings: Deuteronomy 30:15–20; Psalm 1; Luke 9:22–26

The Flesh of Fasting

"Is not this the fast that I choose: to loose the bonds of injustice...to let the oppressed go free?...Is it not to share your bread with the hungry, and bring the homeless into your house?...Then your light shall break forth like the dawn and your healing shall spring up quickly...."
—Isaiah 58:6–8

God of integrity, we cannot mislead you with fasts or sacrifice worn to clothe a deceitful heart. You call us to put flesh on the bones of justice—to recognize companions who hunger; to fill hearts empty of love; to welcome wanderers home, and break the chains of wills that control.

Teach us to see, to gather, to live, and to free. Let your light break open shadows cast by the selfishness of broken promises. Help us to wholeness. Heal what separates us from one another that we might be held by hope in you. Amen.

**As I hunger for the bread of contemplation,
Jesus invites me to the banquet of compassion.**

Readings: Isaiah 58:1–9; Psalm 51; Matthew 9:14–15

Feasting on Conversion

*"The Pharisees and their scribes were complaining to
his disciples saying, 'Why do you eat and drink with
tax collectors and sinners?' Jesus answered,
'Those who are well have no need of a physician, but
those who are sick; I have come to call not the
righteous but sinners to repentance.'"*
—Luke 5:30–32

God of hospitality, you walk with sinners to companion
conversion. You place yourself among the weak and there
invite us to strength. While we pursue our own affairs, you
pursue us with unbounding hope and relentless grace.
Your hand of welcome opens wide and blessings tumble
forth, caught by us, yet called by you to let them slip
through our fingers to become bread and light and healing
for one another.

Continue to spread your table before us, O God. With
Jesus, let us stand at the door and call one another home.
May we find a place in one another that is love and life,
fullness and healing. Amen.

**I know Jesus in the breaking of the bread when
I share my life with another.**

Readings: Isaiah 58:9–14; Psalm 86; Luke 5:27–32

Choices

"One does not live on bread alone, but by every word that comes from the mouth of God."
—Matthew 4:4

God of creation, you formed us in hope and goodness—in your image and likeness. But we struggle to continue the molding of our lives to become worthy of our inheritance... to become worthy of you. Yet will we ever come to be?

Each day we face the choice of good and evil. We try, O God, yet still we are clumsy with this great gift—the freedom that you give us. But sin does not keep you from love. Sin does not keep you from thoughts of salvation. Should we despair of you, you would not despair of us, for you gave us Jesus as our way to life.

Bless our efforts toward good and forgive the times we choose poorly. May Jesus be our bread of life, his Spirit the only power we seek, your holy presence the only value worthy of worship and praise. Amen.

**The dust I was created from and the ashes to which
I will return are sanctuary for the breath of life.**

Readings: Genesis 2:7–9, 3:1–7; Psalm 51; Romans 5:12–19;
Matthew 4:1–11

Holy Communion

"Come, you that are blessed by my Father, inherit the kingdom prepared for you from the foundation of the world; for I was hungry and you gave me food....Truly I tell you, just as you did it to one of the least of these who are members of my family, you did it to me."
—Matthew 25:34–36, 40

Holy God, you are the root of our righteousness...*our rightness*. Out of your holiness, you call us to wholeness. You visit us in one another through integrity of heart. From the center of mystery, you reveal your presence as flesh-in-action.

You draw the thread of communion from being to being, and weave a garment meant to clothe all of human life. No empty show of devotion can replace the embrace of you. Inexhaustible fountain of truth, let the waters that stirred life at baptism carry us along the ways of faith, usher us into the halls of hope, and flood our hearts with love. Amen.

Overwhelmed by the hunger and poverty of the world, I wonder where I will begin. I begin with what I have....I begin with myself.

Readings: Leviticus 19:1–2, 11–18; Psalm 19; Matthew 25:31–46

Crossing Bridges

"Give us this day our daily bread. And forgive us our
debts, as we also have forgiven our debtors."
—Matthew 6:11–12

God of love, we praise your name in Jesus—your Word of Life! He is the seed planted in our hearts from the beginning of time. He is your blessing fallen from the heavens like rain, penetrating roots grounded in you.

Jesus calls us to lift hand and heart to you, who embrace our needs and cradle them in daily bread. He leads us to forgiveness, inviting us across the bridge of alienation to hear wounds that fester far beyond skin-deep...clearing the path to peace with one another.

You know our need for you, O God, before *we* know that need. Turn our minds toward you. Let us focus our day through the lens of your wisdom, that we may know your will like Brailled images present to the touch. Amen.

**When God looks for me at the feast of forgiveness,
will God find me there?**

Readings: Isaiah 55:10–11; Psalm 34; Matthew 6:7–15

Signs and Salvation

"When the crowds were increasing, [Jesus] began to say, 'This generation is an evil generation; it asks for a sign, but no sign will be given to it except the sign of Jonah. For just as Jonah became a sign to the people of Nineveh, so the Son of Man will be to this generation.'"
—Luke 11:29–30

God of forgiveness, we often do what we desire not and grovel in the dust of our own making—slow to raise our eyes to you. Instead you ask us to celebrate sackcloth and ashes, for you are greater than sin and stronger than death.

Help us to live the signs of conversion today: to don sacrifice for sackcloth; to trade action for ashes. Let time cast the sign of prophets in the hearts of our flesh. May we give way to your touch and follow the freedom carved by Christ. Let us use this occasion of grace to celebrate inner strength through the saving courage of Jesus.

**Even when I fail, God does not abandon me;
God leads me to new beginnings.**

Readings: Jonah 3:1–10; Psalm 51; Luke 11:29–32

Providence Provides

"Queen Esther prayed, 'O my Lord, you only are our king; help me, who am alone and have no helper but you....make yourself known in this time of our affliction, and give me courage.'"
—Esther C 14:3, 12

Faithful God, you alone are our help, and so
We pray: Rock of Refuge...give peace as we lean into the ledge of your protection carved for us.
We pray: Rock of Comfort...in whose warm, strong shadow we rest and are refreshed.
We pray: Rock of Safety...whose heights we climb when the shores of life are threatened by troubled waters.
We pray: Rock of Courage...whose steadfast presence enables us to hold on through the night.
We pray: Rock of Wisdom...who allows us to stand on high and sight our world with clearer vision.
We pray: Rock of Solitude...as we thirst for aloneness and drink of your stillness.
We pray...Amen.

**Prayer carries me from doubt to faith,
from hesitancy to confidence.**

Readings: Esther C 14:1, 3–5, 12–15; Psalm 138; Matthew 7:7–12

Gifting One Another

*"So when you are offering your gift at the altar, if you
remember that your brother or sister has something
against you, leave your gift there before the altar and
go; first be reconciled to your brother or sister,
and then come and offer your gift."*
—Matthew 5:23–24

God of justice, the road to reconciliation is a path hard to
tread at times. Vengeance and pride pull us, push us, pre-
vent us even from walking side by side on the way to healing. Time is precious. Let us not squander it searching for
the eye and tooth of self-righteousness. Instead, let us see
one another as gifts...offering forgiveness at your altar.

Let our dignity not come from exacting a price, but
from a sacrifice of love—offered for us by your Son Jesus.
Let this be the prayer that rises from the temple of our
hearts to give you glory. Amen.

Do I really know what is in another's heart?

Readings: Ezekiel 18:21–28; Psalm 130; Matthew 5:20–26

Saturday, *March 19*—
Joseph, Husband of the
Blessed Virgin Mary

Courageous Trust

"Joseph, son of David, do not be afraid to take
Mary as your wife, for the child conceived
in her is from the Holy Spirit."
—Matthew 1:20

Father Joseph, humble bearer of the trust—tender love taught you to embrace the surprise of your promised-one, even though you desired decisions blest by the grace of time.

Father Joseph, humbled by the weight of trust—you offer us wisdom nurtured by an evening's rest, animated by an angel's word and brought to birth through the gift of dreams.

Father Joseph, courageous believer in the trust—you lifted Mary free from the tyranny wrought by wagging tongues and so confirmed the trust, embraced the cost and together received the mystery.

Father Joseph—lover and dreamer, righteous man of God, help us to realize that being human is not an excuse to fall short but a height to be reached as we are challenged to walk humbly with that trust. Amen.

I, too, have been entrusted with God-life.

Readings: 2 Samuel 7:4–5, 12–14, 16; Psalm 89;
Romans 4:13, 16–18, 22; Matthew 1:16, 18–21, 24

Gracing the Ordinary

"Peter said to Jesus, 'Lord, it is good
for us to be here.'"
—Matthew 17:4

God of truth, a blessing you promised and a blessing you give. Through deserts and up mountains, we follow Jesus, and there we find you and ourselves as we are meant to be. We long to hold on to that vision, O God. We try to set up tents and stay as long as we can because it is there that we know we are truly home.

But faith calls us: for it was in faith that Jesus lived life and accepted death. His faith in you was born of love; his love was born of freedom. In Jesus, the bright cloud of your grace is forever upon us. May we be willing to leave the mountaintop experiences of life and walk on the plains of every day. Amen.

Holiness is the freedom to be ordinary.

Readings: Genesis 12:1–4; Psalm 33; 2 Timothy 1:8–10; Matthew 17:1–9

Unconditional Love

*"Forgive, and you will be forgiven; give, and it will
be given to you. A good measure, pressed down,
shaken together, running over, will be put
into your lap; for the measure you give will
be the measure you get back."*
—Luke 6:37–38

God of unconditional love, of freedom beyond-all-measure. How do we fathom within our own hearts a depth of self-giving so much more than our experience? How do we enter your boundless generosity, for we measure not beyond-all-measure?

Help us, O God! Help us to exchange the weight of judgment for the freedom of forgiveness; to clothe our brothers and sisters with the garment of compassion; to let mercy make a home in our hearts and truth the door through which we pass. There, may we enter upon the way of Jesus who is life beyond-all-measure. Amen.

When God throws open the doors to the kingdom, will I question such generosity, or will I welcome all the guests?

Readings: Daniel 9:4–10; Psalm 79; Luke 6:36–38

Tuesday, *March 22*

Servant Freedom

"The greatest among you will be your servant. All who exalt themselves will be humbled, and all who humble themselves will be exalted."
—Matthew 23:11–12

God of truth, you seek us at the heart of what matters. Your gaze goes further than our human eyes. Words are empty unless they frame our faith with flesh. In Jesus, desire and will meet. Truth and justice embrace. Through Jesus, the weight of empty practices was lifted...freedom filled choices and fired sacrifice.

With Jesus, the bonds of pride were broken—and the seat of humility honored. In the spirit of Jesus, then, our vision meets your gaze, our words are made flesh, our desire fires our will and freedom fills all that we embrace—fulfilling your covenant of servant-love. Amen.

I do not "gain" heaven; I grow accustomed to it here on earth—by helping to create it.

Readings: Isaiah 1:10, 16–20; Psalm 50; Matthew 23:1–12

Wednesday, *March 23*

Empowering Humility

"'[Promise me] that these two sons of mine will sit,
one at your right hand and one at your left, in your
kingdom.' But Jesus answered, 'You do not know
what you are asking. Are you able to drink
the cup that I am about to drink?'"
—Matthew 20:21–22

O God, your kingdom is not one of conflict or power, but of kinship. You desire relationship, not rivalry—you empower greatness with humility, and meekness with strength. True places of honor are found in the wounds of your right hand and left hand.

With our brother, Jesus, you bid us gather around and share a cup of blood and tears...to drink before the promised dawn. How foolish we are to think that pushing our way to you avoids the pull of one another. Forgive...forgive us who look for answers in a balance of heaven and earth, but leave no room for the ballast of your wisdom. Forgive us the egos that try to edge you out of our holiness. Amen.

God does not take away conflict or pain. God offers healing within and blessing throughout.

Readings: Jeremiah 18:18–20; Psalm 31; Matthew 20:17–28

Satisfying Hunger

*"There was a rich man who...feasted sumptuously
every day. And at his gate lay a poor man named
Lazarus...who longed to satisfy his hunger with
what fell from the rich man's table."*
—Luke 16:19–21

God of goodness, how many times have we passed through the door of our homes and missed the hungers of you? We know ourselves laden with bread, yet many still cry for mere crumbs. What is wrong with our vision? Why does it tunnel down the paths of our journey but capture only the poor of our choosing? Why are we so narrow in defining needs?

Jesus sensed what could not be seen. He noticed needs in the rhythm of Lazarus' every breath. Teach us through Lazarus to be attentive to our actions, worthy of our words, and generous with our giving...so that another's thirst may reach our own throats and be satisfied by the cooling waters of our compassion. Amen.

I must not separate God from my experience.

Readings: Jeremiah 17:5–10; Psalm 1; Luke 16:19–31

A Moment's Present

"The angel said to her: 'Do not fear, Mary,
for you have found favor with God. And now,
you will conceive in your womb and bear a son,
and you will name him Jesus.'"
—Luke 1:30–31

Mother of God, mother of mystery wrapped in angel-wings, you invite us to hear the Word of God whispered in the womb of our hearts. You show us that presence to the moment unwraps the moment's present.

Mother of God, lady of a love that led you through the darkness of disbelief—you remind us to take time—to rest in the mysteries of human life, for then fear falls away and courage becomes the hand that carries us forth.

Mother of God, keeper of memories yet teacher of what we must release—you share with us the wisdom of honoring the past by weaving it through the tapestry of each day, weeping not over yesterday but wedding it to the hope of tomorrow.

Mother of God, pray for us now and through the hour of our death. Amen.

May I know and practice true devotion to Mary.

Readings: Isaiah 7:10–14, 8:10; Psalm 40; Hebrews 10:4–10; Luke 1:26–38

Compassion

"'I will get up and go to my father.' ...But while he was still far off, his father saw him and was filled with compassion; he ran and put his arms around him and kissed him."
—Luke 15:18, 20

O God, you spread arms of mercy toward us. You embrace us in forgiveness and love. You accept us as we are and allow our wanderings because of freedom's gifts. Yet we are never out of sight for you. Never so far away that your heart cannot beat in rhythm with ours.

Continue to keep us close to you, despite the distance we lay between. Wait to greet us at the moment of our return, for we are often timid, and walk in steps caught up by our guilt.

Help us to realize that you bond us with love...only love. Let that knowing encourage our turning toward home. Amen.

To acknowledge my sin is to celebrate God's mercy....God does not require a pure heart before embracing me.

Readings: Micah 7:14–15, 18–20; Psalm 103;
Luke 15:1–3, 11–32

Image and Likeness

*"Everyone who drinks of this water will be thirsty
again, but those who drink of the water that
I will give them will never be thirsty."*
—John 4:13–14

God of forgiveness, you see us as we truly are—whole yet broken, strong though weak, certain yet still afraid. Sometimes our hearts are dry as stone or hollow as an empty well. You come into our lives to strike the stone and call forth living waters. You fill the well of our lives to over-flowing.

In Jesus, you invite us to find power in weakness and freedom in vulnerability. In Jesus, you drive away false-hood, call for honesty of heart and integrity of spirit. You challenge us to use our gifts rightly and to believe in the grace of your Word. May we die to the image of self that we have carved and be held by the hope of that holiness. Amen.

**God breathed me into life....I am still held in the
image and likeness of God.**

Readings: Exodus 17:3–7; Psalm 95; Romans 5:1–2, 5–8;
John 4:5–42

Acceptance

*"'Truly I tell you, no prophet is accepted in [his]
hometown....There were also many lepers in Israel in
the time of the prophet Elisha, and none of them was
cleansed except Naaman the Syrian.' When they
heard this, all in the synagogue were filled with rage."*
—Luke 4:24, 27–28

O God, who called us to be your own, election is not exclusive—and so we find strangers in the fold of your embrace. Titles are not the seal upon your choice; instead your image printed on the heart of daily living is cause enough. Election embraces faith-in-action.

    Who are we to reject your definition of family and fling aside our brothers and sisters, jealous of your generosity? Open our minds. Free us from the fear that space for others will replace us with you. Open our eyes; lift the veil that values distinction without integrity. May the character of the kingdom be cause enough. Amen.

**Do I doubt the truths of God, or do I fear
what they will mean to my life?**

Readings: 2 Kings 5:1–15; Psalm 42; Luke 4:24–30

Divine Justice

"'Lord, if another member of the church sins against me, how often should I forgive? As many as seven times?' Jesus said to him, 'Not seven times, but, I tell you, seventy–seven times.'"
—Matthew 18:21–22

O God, you created us with the soul of forgiveness. In Jesus, you lead us beyond the limits of winning and losing. You move us from judgment to acceptance and from brokenness to blessing. Your reign is not a system of weights and measures. Your way, instead, finds balance through healing touch.

Draw us to that place of peace when we cannot penetrate the wall between our spirit and our desire—when pain prevents us from making peace with our past. While we may not yet be able to forgive, please forgive for us. You know our desire for homecoming and healing. Help us, then, to open the door to our hearts and to invite the holy in. Amen.

Do I seek permission from God to set limits?

Readings: Daniel 3:25, 34–43; Psalm 25; Matthew 18:21–35

Believing

"[Jesus said to his disciples:] 'Do not think that I have come to abolish the law or the prophets; I have come not to abolish but to fulfill.'"
—Matthew 5:17

God of our fullness, you do not cast away the past to make room for today. Instead, you desire that we mold the flesh of our actions according to the framework of covenant-love, a love built upon foundations cast in the human heart.

Your Word is the thread woven through generations of promise and hope. Old and new meet in your solemn oath of trust and truth. Alpha and Omega embrace in this Word-Made-Flesh. Teach us how to hold the thread long held by the flesh and blood of faith, that we might weave today through the rich garment of yesterday. Amen.

Faith is the "activity" that carries me through my waiting on God.

Readings: Deuteronomy 4:1, 5–9; Psalm 147; Matthew 5:17–19

Invitation to Mystery

*"Now he was casting out a demon that was mute;
when the demon had gone out, the one who had been
mute spoke, and the crowds were amazed....
Others, to test him, kept demanding
from him a sign from heaven."*
—Luke 11:14, 16

God of silence, perhaps what is mute within us is merely your Word-beyond-words. You call forth this Word in Jesus, who loosens tongues to articulate the meaning of faithful love.

The light of daily miracles casts out the darkness and welcomes in the kingdom, for you join us in Jesus. Forgive us when we resist your invitation to accept the mystery of your Word. Enable us to walk each day in the shade of that truth.

Teach us how to live with one another. Do not allow our lack of understanding to be a source of conflict, but the assurance of your presence...a presence beyond our grasp yet within our reach. Amen.

**How do I respond to the miracles God works
in my life? Am I a believer?**

Readings: Jeremiah 7:23–28; Psalm 95; Luke 11:14–23

God–Love

"Jesus answered, '...You shall love the Lord your God with all your heart, and with all your soul, and with all your mind, and with all your strength....You shall love your neighbor as yourself.'"
—Mark 12:29–31

O God, who are one, you call us to yourself through love. Life is the home of your grace. Life is the evidence of your hope in us. You draw us to yourself by touching the places of blessing—the gift of human life. We now lift that gift to you with the hope of holy union.

Bless our hearts with love for you and one another. Inspire our spirits with freedom and devotion. Challenge our minds with truth. Nourish our strength with courage.

Focus our conversion away from fire and ashes...to the burning transformation of *action*, that we might place desire on the altar of experience. Amen.

I was born into the inexhaustible mystery of Love.
I am called to continue that miracle for others.

Readings: Hosea 14:2–10; Psalm 81; Mark 12:28–34

Light and Life

"The Pharisee, standing by himself, was praying thus,
'God, I thank you that I am not like other people:
thieves, rogues, adulterers....' But the tax collector,
standing far off, would not even look up to heaven,
but was beating his breast and saying,
'God, be merciful to me, a sinner!'"
—Luke 18:11, 13

God of light, you penetrate our secret places, not with harshness but with healing. Yet we fear such tenderness, for the rays of your truth would pierce our hearts. At times we stand so strong in self-righteousness that we applaud our goodness and use comparison to others as the stamp of our approval.

You, though, draw the curtain back on our show and introduce a sinner as your beloved. Through the stories of Jesus, you invite us to an honest heart—a heart that embraces limitation and failure as warmly as goodness and success.

Help us, then, to trust that difference does not ensure distinction, and that brokenness *can* be used to build the kingdom. Amen.

Each time I experience my "nothingness,"
my Creator-God says, "Let there be life!"

Readings: Hosea 6:1–6; Psalm 51; Luke 18:9–14

Free to Be Found

*"One thing I do know, that though
I was blind, now I see."*
—John 9:25

God of light and love, you set us free to be found. Free to feel the gaze of God without guilt—without the need to be more than to "be." Free to be found. Free to feel the tenderness that bares the human heart....Where a defense of our sinfulness no longer determines love....Where protest of our imperfection no longer protects us from you.

Free to be found. Free to accept the chasm between creator and creature, knowing it is filled with compassion, for love saves us from the tyranny of ourselves. But will we be saved? Can we allow ourselves to be found? Will we rest within the heart of God without the armor of fear to dress our souls?

Sackcloth and ashes throw us to the ground year after year, O God. How might we touch your truth that is written in the dust...and take the hand that bids us rise? Amen.

Worthiness is not the issue for God. Love is.

Readings: 1 Samuel 16:1, 6–7, 10–13; Psalm 23;
Ephesians 5:8–14; John 9:1–41

The Door of Hope

"Jesus said, 'Unless you see signs and wonders you will not believe.' The official said to him, 'Sir, come down before my little boy dies.' Jesus said to him, 'Go; your son will live.' The man believed the word that Jesus spoke to him and started on his way."
—John 4:48–50

God of possibilities, we look for *proof*—desiring to be dazzled by signs and wonders. You, instead, seek *faith*—calling us to believe in your Word. That Word became flesh and carried us beyond promise to abundant life.

We seek healing today in the gift of faith that leads us down the road to Jesus. *Faith that casts out fear. Faith that opens the door to hope*. Pour this gift of faith, O God, into hearts that are broken by cynicism. Let the sign of this weakness of ours be the place that bears the seal of your love. Amen.

Belief is the choice I make between meaninglessness and mystery.

Readings: Isaiah 65:17–21; Psalm 30; John 4:43–54

Seeking Wholeness

"Jesus said, 'Do you want to be made well?' The sick man answered him, 'Sir, I have no one to put me into the pool when the water is stirred up....'"
—John 5:6–7

God of healing, we come to you in pieces at times—unable to hear your word, walk in your ways, or hope for what is beyond the human eye. We desire healing but know that by ourselves we are unable to risk that leap of freedom into your waiting arms.

Have mercy, then, and lift us. Carry us, O God, more deeply into the waters of our baptism. Drown us in grace, that we may have life through the breath of your Spirit.

Keep us willing in hope, carefree in faith, and waiting on your love. Amen.

**God is not discouraged with me even when
I am discouraged with myself.**

Readings: Ezekiel 47:1–9, 12; Psalm 46; John 5:1–16

Family Living

*"Jesus said to them, 'I tell you, the Son can
do nothing on his own, but only what
he sees the Father doing....'"*
—John 5:19

O God, who holds us warmly in a parent's love....Today we desire to draw upon the bountiful legacy of that love. Our brother, Jesus, understood the richness of this relationship. He lived under the blessing of belonging to you.

Your love lets go and allows us to choose the places where we may grow. But sometimes we lack right judgment. It is then that we look to you and ask for a will in keeping with our desires.

Give us the mind of Christ that was fashioned by the Holy Spirit, and a heart that knows the loving wisdom of your will. Amen

The Incarnation is the divine embrace of human limitation.

Readings: Isaiah 49:8–15; Psalm 145; John 5:17–30

The Grace of Desire

"He was a burning and shining lamp, and you were willing to rejoice for a while in his light. But I have a testimony greater than John's....I have come in my Father's name, and you do not accept me...."
—John 5:35–36, 43

God of unbelievers, we *want* to believe but it is hard for us to *trust* what we do not see. You knew that need and embraced our unbelief in Jesus, who sought sinners and loved us into truth.

Give us, then, the love of your son, who clothed his words in flesh; the courage of your son, who raised the burning lamp of John to light the horizon of life itself; the faith of your son, who poured himself into the chalice of human suffering to shatter its darkness forever.

O God, fill us with faith that will carry us beyond the waters of our baptism that we, too, may be love, light and life. Amen.

Faith lives in the quiet corners of desire.

Readings: Exodus 32:7–14; Psalm 106; John 5:31–47

Respecting the Moment

"Jesus went about in Galilee...because the Jews were looking for an opportunity to kill him. Now the Jewish festival of Booths was near....But after his brothers had gone to the festival, then he also went, not publicly but as it were in secret."
—John 7:1–2, 10

God of time, you teach us to respect the hour, the moment...for an epiphany might go unnoticed, if we were not to watch for stars.

For Jesus, time was sacred....With Jesus, may we live in this rhythm of breath-by-breath and freely ride the pendulum of yet another grace. Save us from fear that would take time captive, causing us to cling to its fruit long after the ripening.

Teach us to hold the moment *lightly*, that we might not impose upon it meaning it does not hold. May we recognize each day as an opportunity, be moved by the color-cry of dawn, and greet the grace that time hopes for us. Amen.

Do I ask, "What is around me to keep me safe?" or "Who is within me?"

Readings: Wisdom 2:1, 12–22; Psalm 34; John 7:1–2, 10, 25–30

Unseeing Yet Perceiving

"'Surely the Messiah does not come from Galilee, does he? Has not the scripture said that the Messiah is descended from David and comes from Bethlehem, the village where David lived?' So there was a division in the crowd because of him."
—John 7:41–43

O God, forever free of our theories and ideas, you challenge the limits we place on you in the person of Jesus. There you are not to be grasped. Instead we are invited to dream dreams and seek possibilities, for life leads us to Jesus and what we seek *can* be found.

Protect us from the blindness of cynicism. Give us a vision that permits decisions of the heart. Continue to elude us when defining you is only for our comfort. Our minds, for all their wonder, can build enclosures that trap creative-joy.

Let us lift the gift of your presence free of our attachments, and rise to the surprise of grace. Amen.

**The fire of the Holy Spirit purifies my vision so that
I can see clearly that God is mystery.**

Readings: Jeremiah 11:18–20; Psalm 7; John 7:40–53

Wrapped in Darkness

*"This illness does not lead to death; rather
it is for God's glory, so that the Son of God
may be glorified through it."*
—John 11:4–5

Out of the depths we cry to you, O God: the depths of our doubts and disbelief; the depths of our fears and vulnerability; the depths of the tomb we carve into the fabric of our lives—bound like Lazarus, wrapped in darkness like a seed. The words of Jesus echo in our ears: *to die is to live, to lose is to find*.

Cradle the seed of our lives in your hand, O God. Help us to befriend the holy ground of life that we might not resist the plunge into its darkness. Let us fall lightly that we might greet the dying with the certainty of new life.

Let us remember your time in the tomb, but also that you come as sure as the dawn to shatter the stone and call us forth unbound and free. Amen.

I know my longing for God, but do I realize God's longing for me?

Reading: Ezekiel 37:12–14; Psalm 130; Romans 8:8–11;
John 11:1–45

Revealing Light

*"Jesus said to her, 'Woman, where are they? Has no
one condemned you?' She said, 'No one, sir.'
And Jesus said, 'Neither do I condemn you.
Go your way, and from now on do not sin again.'"*
—John 8:10–11

O God, who finds us hiding in our own shadows, through
Jesus you extend a hand of hope inviting us to step into
your revealing light—a light that anoints wounds long-
hidden by fear and shame.

We resist those who bind and drag us from darkness
into day, for their harshness throws us at the feet of judgment. Instead, you trace words of light upon our hearts.
Lead us, then, by love that we may find the treasure of
ourselves, lift it before the eyes of Jesus, and with him
say: Holy....Holy....Holy. Amen.

**I must gather the past and broken things to
discover the grace of today.**

Readings: Daniel 13:1–9, 15–17, 19–30, 33–62;
Psalm 23; John 8:1–11

Tuesday, *April 12*

Willing Faith

*"When you have lifted up the Son of Man,
then you will realize that I am he, and that
I do nothing on my own, but I speak these
things as the Father instructed me."*
—John 8:28

God of patience, we often come before you seeking
answers already wrapped within your Word. The untiring
heart of Jesus holds our questions until faith finds us willing to walk beyond our needs. With Jesus, we climb the
wood, open our arms and outstretch our feet.

We welcome the flow of water and blood—longing to
be washed in Spirit and in Truth in his soul and divinity.

May the source of our lives and the healer of our
souls embrace us in his final sigh; for that moment, his
last breath, stirred the first breath of our lives. Amen.

**Many times I know the cross that I carry. But how
has this cross carried me—to new life?**

Readings: Numbers 21:4–9; Psalm 102; John 8:21–30

The Human Heart

*"Then Jesus said to the Jews who had believed in him,
'If you continue in my word, you are truly my
disciples; and you will know the truth,
and the truth will make you free.'"*
—John 8:31–32

God of courage, we anticipate your Spirit in the words of Jesus today. Freedom and truth kiss the fire of life. But fear fires obstinate hearts, and words of life are unmet sparks. Help us to lift fear from our shoulders and throw it off the edges of this earth. Let it fall into its own orbit, perhaps encircling us but never again crashing down and crushing us to the pulp of unbelief.

Your truth does *not* teach with violence. Your freedom intends our healing. Be with us, O God. Help us cast out fear by love, by grace...by *you*. Lift us out of the depths of our unknown thirsts into the fullness of freedom and life. Amen.

God is held captive by the struggles of the human heart.

Readings: Daniel 3:14–20, 91–92, 95; Daniel 3:52–56;
John 8:31–42

The Wideness of Mercy

*"Very truly, I tell you, whoever keeps
my word will never see death."*
—John 8:51

God of the living, your Word spoke life. In Jesus, you parted the veil of time that we might know beyond-our-wildest-dreams. But will we ever *comprehend* this new life? Will death forever be the mystery that blurs our vision, preventing us from fathoming life's fullness?

Let the wideness of your mercy be upon us, O God. Receive our questions. Give us courage to walk with them into eternal day. When fear frightens us, call us to the feet of your Word-Made-Flesh and there set us free.

Call us forth unbound that we may leave the tomb of our terrors with hope...in the resurrected life. Amen.

**Wherever I taste death and long for new life, it is
precisely there that Jesus bids me: "Come forth."**

Readings: Genesis 17:3–9; Psalm 105; John 8:51–59

Expectations

"'It is not for a good work that we are going to stone you, but for blasphemy, because you, though only a human being, are making yourself God.' Jesus answered..., 'If I am not doing the works of my Father, then do not believe me. But if I do them...believe the works, so that you may know and understand that the Father is in me and I am in the Father.'"
—John 10:33, 37–39

O God, your Word-Made-Flesh shattered our notions of Messiah and challenged our concept of the kingdom. Jesus held your face before us and smiled. The wrappings of mystery meant to draw us near became a cloak for cynicism and disbelief instead. Many walked away, praying for the dreamer...the blasphemer.

O God, slow our steps. Do not allow us to walk away from your Son. When the truth falls hard upon our hearts, help us to find the impossible possible. Help us to *trust* in Jesus and to descend willingly into the Mystery that wraps us round in love. Amen.

When I pray that God may show me the way, do I sometimes miss the person or situation God sends me?

Readings: Jeremiah 20:10–13; Psalm 18; John 10:31–42

Fear and Disbelief

"So the chief priests and the Pharisees called a meeting
of the council, and said, '...If we let him go on like
this, everyone will believe in him....' So from that day
on they planned to put him to death."
—John 11:47–48, 53

God of the prophets, Jesus was the lamb of sacrifice whose blood sealed your covenant love. Why did fear generate disbelief, when only wonder and forgiveness flowed from Jesus? Destruction worked its way into the human heart when mystery could not be grasped.

Forgive us our fears, today, when we use them to choose rejection of what we do not understand. The abandon of Jesus to our human limitations is much too much for our minds *and* hearts to hold.

Fill our flesh with the fullness of the Spirit that faith may lead us beyond ourselves to the blessings of our unknowing. Amen.

It is a flash of God-Light that changes blindness into blessing.

Readings: Ezekiel 37:21–28; Jeremiah 31:10–13; John 11:45–56

Passionate Love

"You will all become deserters because of me this night; for it is written, 'I will strike the shepherd, and the sheep of the flock will be scattered.'"
—Matthew 26:31

Jesus, you embraced abandonment by those who called you "Teacher" and "Lord" and accepted the cross without question or condemnation.…May we embrace those who no longer have need for us, those who leave our lives.

Jesus, you surrendered to ignorance, humiliation, and injustice.…May we surrender our need for approval and understanding.

Jesus, you died alone, hanging against the sky, crying out, fearing your Father-God had forgotten you.…May we cry out with love when fear and isolation threaten our lives.

Jesus, in the end, you gave over your body and spirit to the God we could not see.…Savior and Lord, in the end, may we bow our human minds to divine wisdom, give our bodies to sacrificial love, and place our spirits in holy union with you…our act of faith in the God we cannot see. Amen.

**Jesus endured humiliation, injustice, pain, and death—
He loved me with a passion.**

Readings: Matthew 21:1–11; Isaiah 50:4–7; Psalm 22; Philippians 2:6–11; Matthew 26:14—27:66

Redeeming Darkness

"Mary took a pound of costly perfume...anointed
Jesus' feet, and wiped them with her hair....Jesus said,
'Leave her alone. She bought it so that she might
keep it for the day of my burial....'"
—John 12:3, 7

O God, in you darkness and light are the same. I pray then that you abide with me in the shadows. Become the cloak of darkness that wraps my steps so that frustration and fear might not harm me in this journey of night. For doubt drags my feet and questions disquiet my soul.

Jesus, my resurrection and life, let my blindness not hide me from you. Rather, redeem the darkness I sometimes live in. Transform the stumbling block of doubt into a stepping-stone of strength as I walk on the waters of my baptism.

Uphold my steps by faith. Guide my heart through hope. Consecrate my path through love. May my death to this life be the birth of soul-fire that leads me to you. Amen.

I face death much like a story reaching a conclusion
or resolution, for death is the threshold to
eternal resolution...to God.

Readings: Isaiah 42:1–7; Psalm 27; John 12:1–11

Remembering Jesus

*"Peter said to him, 'Lord, why can I not follow you
now? I will lay down my life for you.' Jesus answered,
'Will you lay down your life for me? Very truly,
I tell you, before the cock crows, you will
have denied me three times.'"*
—John 13:37–38

God of my existence, hold me firm in the ways of Jesus.
Draw me down into the ground of love where you are
rooted in the human heart. Yet lift me from the earth of
my ego-dwelling; set me free from selfish concern. Fix
faith in my soul that will hold me fast...for life may lead me
to places I do not wish to go.

Cast the memory of Jesus as bread along the way.
Then what I fear as mere crumbs becomes a banquet—a
wisdom of heart, the cost of loving. Amen.

**When I am finally called home, will I face God, able to say:
"I know in whom I have believed"?**

Readings: Isaiah 49:1–6; Psalm 71; John 13:21–33, 36–38

God of My Heart

"Judas said, 'What will you give me if I betray him to you?' They paid him thirty pieces of silver. And from that moment he began to look for an opportunity to betray him."
—Matthew 26:15–16

God of my heart, give me the humility to surrender to you, for my prayer is often an act of faith—believing without seeing, trusting without knowing, loving without feeling.

God of my heart, yesterday and tomorrow lie in balance. May I not measure myself by the past, nor fracture myself by the future. God of all that makes me *me*, keep me from burdening others with my ideals. Gift me with your words but teach me how to listen.

And when I come to the edge of this life, throw open the doors to my deepest desire and bid me fly into your fullness....O God of my heart. Amen.

By his stripes we are healed. Each time I embrace the wounds of the whip, I meet the place of my healing.

Readings: Isaiah 50:4–9; Psalm 69; Matthew 26:14–25

Life through Death

"Jesus answered, 'You do not know now what I am doing, but later you will understand.'"
—John 13:7

Father, this meal is my last supper—I feel it in my bones. My flesh prepares a three-day fast. Doom weighs heavy on me now, and yet I am called to celebrate both slavery and freedom.

My friends prepare a table for me in the sight of all my foes. Father, I close my eyes and see the end of my journey. So soon, Father, so soon? I know they are gathering now in the streets outside our dinner room. I know that, Father; I know.

I go now to celebrate your love for us. I go to remember the gift and to *become* the gift. I go to pass over from slavery to freedom today. I go to share food and become bread. I go to declare that the chains of bondage are broken. I go to become broken.

Your will be done, Father...and be there with me in the doing. Amen.

The grain of wheat must willingly fall to the ground.

Readings: Exodus 12:1–8, 11–14; Psalm 116; 1 Corinthians 11:23–26; John 13:1–15

Mystery of New Life

"[Jesus] went out to what is called The Place of the
Skull...Golgotha. There they crucified him, and with
him two others...with Jesus between them."
—John 19:17–18

Death is all around me. Father, *have* you forsaken me?
Have they? I thirst...are you enough to quench my need?

You are source and satisfaction. How does that
plumb the depths of my well today? My bones are num-
bered, dry and brittle each time I hang from this cross.
When I commend my spirit, at the end, will you be there
to catch and capture it? How will I sink into the inexhaustible mystery of you?

If you are love, and we meet on the other side, will I
keep on loving? Will this new flesh reach into you and back
across the other side? Will I continue to co-create, to build
the kingdom, to rescue the poor, to lift hearts, to affect
life, to effect life, to touch the earth?

Father, into your hands I commend my spirit. Amen.

For Jesus, this moment was an act of faith—
faith in the power of light over darkness.

Readings: Isaiah 52:13–53:12; Psalm 31;
Hebrews 4:14–16, 5:7–9; John 18:1—19:42

The Blessings of God

*"Do not be afraid; I know that you are looking for
Jesus who was crucified. He is not here;
for he has been raised."*
—Matthew 28:5–6

Holy Night...
Holy Light, burn deeply in my soul. Hallow the tomb of
   my flesh so that freedom may laugh where bondage
   once wept.
Holy Night...
Holy Light, pour your healing word, the Yes-of-God
   into wounds left dark and deep—aching with desire
   for this anointing.
Holy Night...
Holy Light, cast rays of grace into my night. Let them
   seek the corners of my heart where hides the fear
   of my shadowland.
Holy Night...
Holy Light, carry me across the threshold of joy-at-
   dawn, that day will find love leading me to life.
   Amen.

I must live my brokenness under the blessing of God.

Readings: Genesis: 1:1—2:2; Genesis 22:1–18;
Exodus 14:15—15:1; Exodus 15:1–18; Isaiah 54:5–14;
Isaiah 55: 1–11; Baruch 3:9–15, 32—4:4; Ezekiel 36:16–28;
Romans 6:3–11; Psalm 118; Matthew 28:1–10

Jesus, the Christ

*"Mary Magdalene came to the tomb and saw
that the stone had been removed."*
—John 20:1

Laughter echoes in the tomb,
fills the hollows and rolls away the stone
that separates the heart of humankind
from knowing the heart of God.

The song of birds greets the laughter—
blending with it and plays with the melody
of joy-in-the-morning.

Wrappings of yesterday are left as memories,
reminders of what was
and what will be...for us.
But empty grave and open doorway
hold the laughter that will follow
for we, too,
will leave yesterday behind.

**When I pray for peace that the world cannot give, I must
remember it is a peace that the world cannot take away.**

Readings: Acts 10:34, 37–43; Psalm 118;
Colossians 3:1–4; John 20:1–9

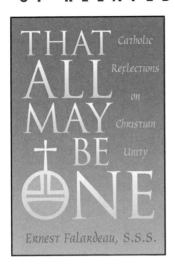

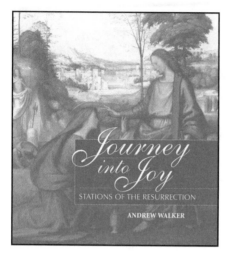

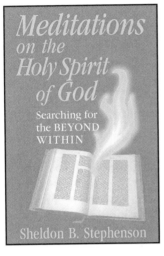

**Meditations on the
Holy Spirit of God**
*Searching for the
Beyond Within*

Sheldon B. Stephenson

Forty-nine meditations appropriate for use especially
between Easter and Pentecost that connect the Holy
Spirit to the life of Christians.

ISBN: 0-8091-3833-6   Price $8.95

*(Price and availability
subject to change)*

Ask at your local bookstore.

*For more information or to get a
free catalog of our publications, contact us at:*

Paulist Press · 997 Macarthur Boulevard · Mahwah, NJ 07430
1-800-218-1903 · Fax: 1-800-836-3161
E-mail: info@paulistpress.com
Visit our website at www.paulistpress.com

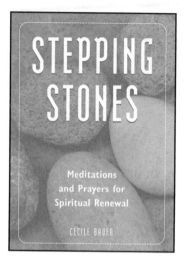

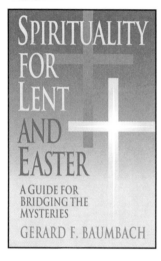

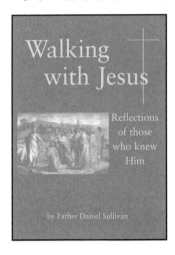

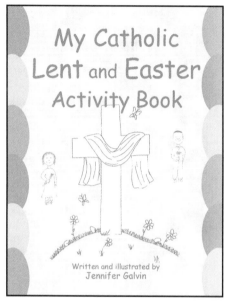

Makes a Great Gift!

Living the Days of Lent 2012

Paulist's best-selling series of daily Lenten devotions uses scripture, prose reflections, and original prayers and poems to center readers' minds and souls and gently bring them to readiness for Easter. With these daily meditations, readers learn to open themselves to the risks and rewards of living a fuller life, of finding compassion from themselves and others, and of resting more deeply in God's loving care.

Living the Days of Lent 2012—
- runs daily from Ash Wednesday through Easter Sunday.
- ends each day's selection with the daily lectionary citations.
- includes pointed challenges for one's thoughts and actions.
- comes in a tear-out, page-a-day format for handy use.

-------------------------------- *Reserve Your Copy Today!* --------------------------------

Please send me _____ copy(ies) of: **Living the Days of Lent 2012 #978-0-8091-4711-3** @ **$4.95 ea.**

Please include applicable sales tax, and postage and handling ($3.50 for first $20 plus 50¢ for each additional $10 ordered)—check or money order only payable to **Paulist Press.**

Enclosed is my check or money order in the amount of $ _____

Name _____

Position _____

Institution _____

Street _____

City/State/Zip _____

Phone # _____

For more information or to receive a free catalog of our publications, contact us at:

 Paulist Press™ 997 Macarthur Blvd., Mahwah, N.J. 07430 • 1-800-218-1903
FAX 1-800-836-3161 • E-MAIL: info@paulistpress.com • www.paulistpress.com
Prices subject to change without notice.